Follow Chic Online

@chicinfluencer

Listen

Direct Sales Done Right Podcast

this PLANNER BELONGS TO

_____

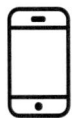

Share your Direct Sales Done Right Plans with us on
social media by tagging us @chicinfluencer #DirectSalesDoneRight
Tell us how your planner is changing your business strategy.

To get more tips from us you can also subscribe
to the Direct Sales Done Right podcast on iTunes, Spotify,
Soundcloud, or anywhere you can download podcasts.

Second Edition

Copyright © 2022 Chic Influencer
chicinfluencer.com

All rights reserved.
ISBN: 978-1-7359727-3-2

No part of this book may be reproduced or transmitted in any form or by any means, electronic or mechanical, including photocopying, recording or by an information storage and retrieval system – except by a reviewer who may quote brief passages in a review to be printed in a magazine, newspaper or on the Web – without permission in writing from the publisher.

Design by Margaret Cogswell | www.margaretcogswell.com

DIRECT SALES DONE RIGHT ACADEMY

The academy is the foundation for doing direct sales right. The academy gives you the strategies and tools to build a successful business. The academy is a community that it will teach you tracking, conversations, social media, follow-ups, and handling objections. This is where you get everything you need for success in direct sales! This is your one-stop shop for building a successful direct sales business.

Membership Includes:

- 5 core lessons to build a successful direct sales business
- Weekly live trainings for direct sales business owners
- Monthly resources (downloadables) exclusive to the Direct Sales Done Right academy students
- Lifetime access to recordings and resources
- Access to a collaborative members-only Facebook Community
- Social media best practices for direct sellers
- Tools and strategies to write social media content

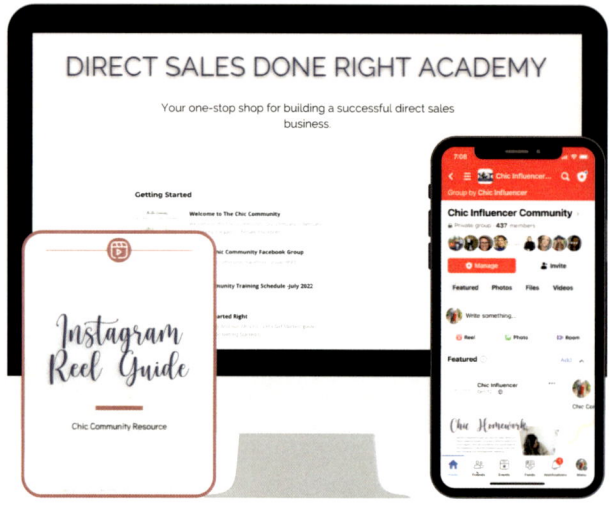

Kayla O.

The Academy has been so beneficial helping me to **feel more confident with my conversations**. Through learning to listen more than I speak, I've really been able to help make recommendations truly based on what the person wants and not just on what I've been trained to lead with or sell. The level of customer service that I'm providing now is so much better because of my investment in this course. I'm always striving to give the Chic level customer experience!! **I doubled my income** in the couple of months from DSDR versus the entire first 4 months of the year!

Jen W.

I loved DSDR! Really each of the courses I've taken and joining the Chic community has been a game changer for my personal and business confidence. I love the way Katy & Melanie approach Direct Sales and teaching us how to build a business we love and make an impact we can be proud of! I have **more personal confidence** in myself, **getting specific about who I want to help most and why**, being more bold and direct in invites once relationships have been built and just focusing on the activity, not the outcome. The most helpful thing for me has been **niching down** and really learning how to speak directly to my ideal person (not a wide cast) and be more intentional to post with purpose.

Robyn B.

I am now getting out there more and more. **I feel more confident with my posting** and with myself in general. I've even posted about the business opportunity, which I have never done before. I am **having conversations** and **adding new followers**. I am now beginning to do some tracking of my insights on Facebook and IG, which I never did before. Both of my accounts are now creator / professional. Before this Academy, I was literally scrambling, felt at a loss and was going to quit. I love the community I am a part of, and that really saddened me. I'm thankful I was given the opportunity to join this community.

Join the course!

SAVE 10% WITH CODE: DSDR10PLANNER

ROCKSTAR RECRUITMENT COURSE

The most comprehensive direct sales program for identifying, attracting, and enrolling the right team members to your network marketing business. Melanie will guide you every step of the way to confidently build your team!

By the end of the course you will have:

- The mindset required to be a confident recruiter for your direct sales business.
- The formula for developing a healthy pipeline so that you never run out of people to invite.
- A clearly defined system for using social media to showcase your business.
- A step-by-step guide for how to set up, execute, and enroll team members through business opportunity events.
- A step-by-step guide for how to implement a back end email marketing strategy for collecting leads, nurturing, and enrolling new and excited team members.
- Confidence in conversations about the business opportunity, sharing the opportunity, asking people to enroll, and completing the sign up process.

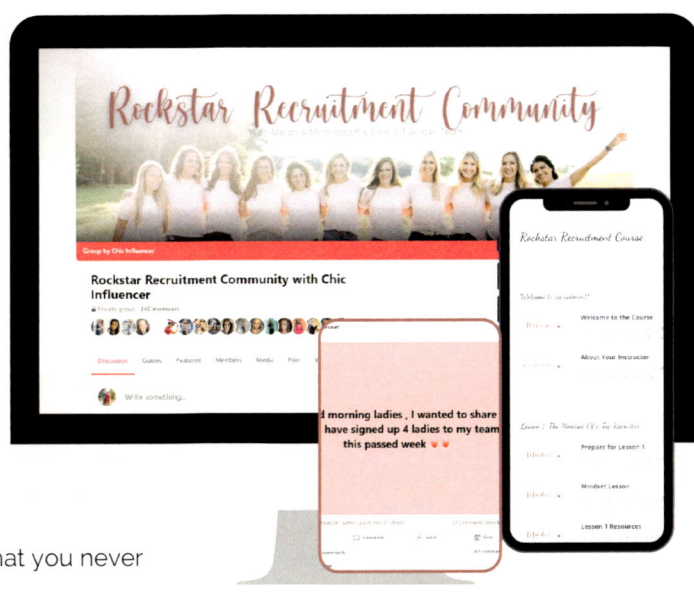

SCAN ME

Join the course!

SAVE 10% WITH CODE: RECRUIT10PLANNER

In the first 8 months of 2022, I recruited 6 new members to my team. After joining the Rockstar Recruitment Course, **I added 13 new team members** in the final 4 months of the year! The difference for me was tweaking the way I was doing things because you can think you are doing things the way you should, but a simple tweak can change everything.

Lacey H.

I hesitated to sign up for this course because I have been in the business for so long, but this truly helped me to reignite my fire and start to find the up-and-coming leaders on my team that I've been searching for. They are right in front of me. I just wasn't speaking directly to them or showing them how I could help. Now, I can CONFIDENTLY do that, and I am so excited to continue to implement the systems I learned to then pass on to my team so they can do the same.

Brooke C.

By the 2nd week of the course, I had already **recruited 3 WORKING coaches** who are actually showing up and doing things alongside me! This course quite possibly will be the catalyst to an incredible year for my now-growing team.

CHIC BRANDING EXPERIENCE

The Chic Branding Experience clarifies your unique brand story. This customized experience consists of 4 phases designed to create a completely unique marketing strategy for your intentional brand.

Investment Includes:

- In-depth audit and analysis of your Instagram account
- 1-hour branding session with Katy Ursta via Zoom
- Comprehensive, customized branding & and marketing guide (PDF) designed specifically for your intentional brand
- 30-minute optimization session via Zoom with your personally assigned Social Media Specialist
- One month of guidance and support during the first stage of implementation

Dawn C.

Because of the Chic Branding Experience, I understand who I am creating content for, I no longer struggle with coming up with content and I have a clear vision of my **intentional brand**. I've learned how to craft a staple story that conveys why and what I do. I think my audience totally knows what to expect when they come to my account. Here are some numbers: when I started working with (Chic), I was almost at my 1 year with Hugh and Grace and was stagnant in my rank. The month I worked with you guys, **I ranked up, and my sales more than doubled from where I was at the same time last year.** I have been asked to go live on 3 other accounts, who found me through my Instagram. Although initially my followers went down as I was niching, **I have increased my followers by over 1,500, and my engagement is up as well.**

Shannon S.

The Chic Branding Experience really opened my eyes to look at my IG from a follower's perspective. I changed how I began a post by creating better hooks and CTA. I didn't change the focus of what I was doing or who I am, but it is presented much more clearly on my **IG to grab attention and connect with my ideal audience**. My following **increased by 80K in only 3 months** after implementing these changes. I not only just grew my following, but my followers are my ideal customers!

Missy T.

I am ready to shift my focus on my team a bit more. **I signed up 4 new distributors over the last 45 days.** They are already running with it!! And some of my others that had been laying low have come back into action. It's really nice to see the work come to fruition. Thanks for always cheering me on. It helps me!

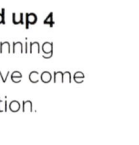

MORE ON THE *Branding Experience* HERE!

SAVE $100 WITH CODE: CBE100PLANNER

6 MONTH LEADERSHIP MASTERMIND

An upper-level mentorship program that supports leaders in getting organized, decreasing overwhelm, creating a systematic approach to their businesses, and duplicating the process throughout their organization.

Mastermind Includes:

- Bi-monthly 90-minute sessions with training and discussion, plus actionable steps
- Whats App chat for collaboration, support, and motivation
- Dozens of resources for leaders that Melanie Mitro has developed and implemented effectively
- Lifetime access to all documents, resources, and recordings

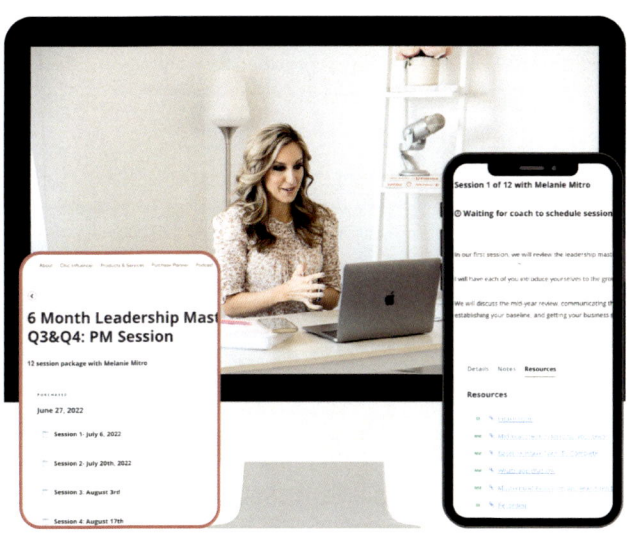

Lauren H.

I have seen so many amazing changes to my business this year. I have **learned how to incorporate systems for onboarding**, systems for new artists to learn to be successful, and systems in place to help our leaders learn to duplicate. **I have also recruited more new artists in a 3 month time frame, than I have in a year.** Melanie has also taught me how to set boundaries as a leader, so not only can I be successful in my own personal business, but a more present mom and wife as well. Since signing up for the Leadership Mastermind, **I have become a more confident leader** and feel like I now have the tools to be more successful in my own business and as a leader raising other new leaders on my own team. Melanie is so inspirational and has so much knowledge in this business. Her organization and her incredible way of teaching systems have **challenged me to think differently** and **implement new strategies** to help raise my business to another level.

Heather O.

I am currently a Millionaire Team Member with Herbalife. Since beginning the Leadership Mastermind with Melanie, I have **seen an increase of 50,000+ in sales** from my organization (team). I have received some amazing tools and structures to help me **get better organized** and **lead my team to success**. We have taken on more coaches to our team from January to April than we did all last year, 2022. I do this business side by side with my husband. And he loves hearing Melanie speak and uses her tools and podcasts as well!! Melanie is truly such an amazing person and such an inspirational leader. I love and enjoy all of the time we spend with her, and when driving, I listen to her podcasts on repeat. During the Leadership Mastermind, I was also able to get four of my team members to sign up for the Rockstar Recruitment Course that launched as well!! So my team believes just as much as I do that these courses are important!!

Madeline G.

I have **gained 22 new executives** on my team and **42 new people entering into qualifications** since joining the Leadership Mastermind!

DIRECT SALES DONE RIGHT BOOK & OFFICIAL WORKBOOK

Not seeing results when you follow the advice of industry leaders, company training, and even your well-meaning mentors? Maybe you've been wrestling with your own doubts and fears. Perhaps you've lost your initial spark, sitting stagnant instead of growing toward your goals. Maybe you've created the vision board and taken action, but it still feels like something is missing.

In this honest and action-oriented guide, Katy Ursta, a successful direct seller with over eleven years of network marketing experience, presents a proven plan to stop wasting time and start making meaningful money.

Scan the QR to buy the book!

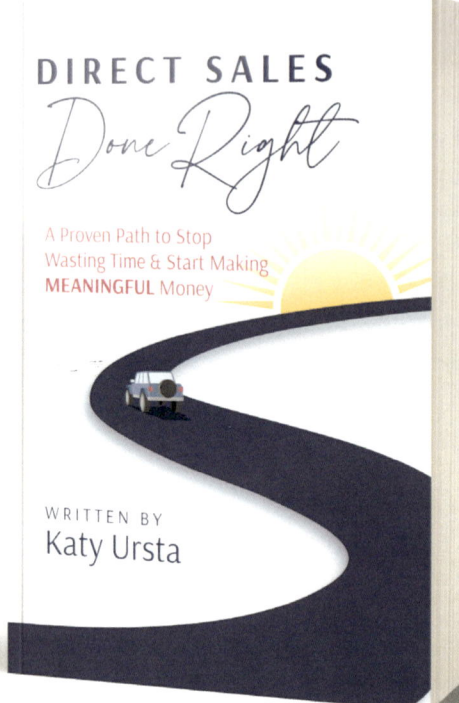

The workbook is designed to support your journey while reading *Direct Sales Done Right*. Meticulously curated by Katy Ursta and Melanie Mitro of Chic Influencer this is the only approved workbook to accompany the *Direct Sales Done Right* book.

Scan the QR to buy the workbook!

SUBSCRIBE TODAY!

DIRECT SALES DONE RIGHT
Podcast

Grab a cup of coffee; let's talk direct sales done right!

LET'S STAY CONNECTED!

 Chic Influencer

 @katywritescontent
@melaniemitro
@chicinfluencer

 @chicinfluencer

 support@chicinfluencer.com

Table of Contents

The Story Behind the Planner   9

Introduction   12

SOCIAL MEDIA DONE RIGHT   15

VISION CASTING DONE RIGHT   29

GOAL SETTING DONE RIGHT   35

PLANNING DONE RIGHT   47
    Reflect & Refine   49
    IPA Tracker   52
    Weekly Social Media Plan   57
    End of Month Reflection   64

CONFETTI   356

THE STORY BEHIND THE PLANNER

Meet Your Direct Sales Done Right Mentors

We couldn't be more excited to help you grow your following, and more importantly, share your message with people who can connect with your story! It's so nice to meet you here behind the scenes of your social media page. We know how much heart and time you put into your direct sales business. We also know how frustrating it can be when you feel like you are doing all the right things, but it's not connecting with your audience. Our vision is to help you simplify your social strategy and clarify your specific marketing message through an easy-to-use social media planner. You'll find resources, content starters, weekly planning and reflection, brainstorming activities, and online trainings, as well as a collaborative Facebook group.

Let's do this!

Make sure you stay connected!

We want to see how you are using your planner. Tag us @chicinfluencer using **#directsalesdoneright** and let us know what you think!

Please also join others using the Direct Sales Done Right Planner on Facebook at: **facebook.com/groups/directsalesdonerightplanner**

SCAN ME!

Hey friends!

I am Katy Ursta, and I have 11 years in the direct sales (network marketing) industry. During the early years of building my business, I was juggling a full time job as a seventh grade Reading teacher and raising my son. When I was only a few months into growing my business, I gave birth to my second son. Within months, I was diagnosed with stage 4 cancer. During that time I started using my Facebook account as a way to cope with the diagnosis and the battle by writing. The more I shared my story, the more I connected with others to sweat and to move their body, not because they have to but because they *get to*. Cancer shifted the way I approached my business and helped me clarify my vision. My direct sales business grew over 300% during that time and it wasn't because I was doing "more" or had a secret formula to success. I was just consistently conveying a message that connected my audience to my mission in direct sales.

In the past few years, my work has been featured on *The Today Show, Today Parents, Love What Matters*, and *Her View From Home*. In 2020, I published *The Back Pocket Prayer Journal* for women who, like me, wonder if they are "Jesus-ing wrong". In 2023, I released *Direct Sales Done Right: A Proven Path to Stop Wasting and Start Making Meaningful Money*. I've built a career alongside my personal direct sales sponsor, Melanie Mitro, through our company Chic Influencer.

We support women in the direct sales industry through resources, online courses, community, and, of course, writing content that builds connections. When I am not writing content, you will likely find me at the hockey rink cheering on my sons, Nick (13) and Dom (10).

Come hang out with me on Instagram @katywritescontent or on Facebook at facebook.com/onefitfighter

Hey there!

Melanie Mitro here! I am married to my husband, Matt, and we have two boys who are keeping us really busy in this season of life.

I am the former Director of an Early Intervention Program that served clients from birth to age three. After the birth of my first son, I left my full-time career to be a stay-at-home mom. I was introduced to network marketing when I was searching for a solution to get rid of the post-baby weight. In July of 2011, I launched my network marketing business with the vision of helping other mommas gain their bodies back after kids.

I have been in the network marketing industry for the past eleven years. I went from being a stay-at-home mom to the top distributor in the company in three years, creating a multi-seven figure income using social media as my primary source of marketing. I served on the Coach Advisory Board for the company, and in 2018 I was given the CEO Award. I have a passion for teaching women in direct sales how to strategically market their businesses through social media to drive results. I also love helping women develop systems, build thriving and successful downlines, step into their leadership roles, duplicate their success, and scale their businesses to give them freedom and purpose that aligns to their core values. I have spoken on stage for leadership conferences, annual conventions, and local events.

When I'm not focusing on my business, I'm either watching my two boys play basketball, baseball, or snuggled up on the couch with the family watching a movie. I have a tough love approach to business and I want nothing more than to see my people succeed.

You can find more of my social media content on Instagram @melaniemitro or on facebook.com/melaniemitro

INTRODUCTION

It's time to do Direct Sales Right! Are you ready?!

We see you over there, typing away in the early mornings, working on your dreams with a cup of coffee in hand and tired eyes that haven't yet peeled open completely.

We see you over there, working late into the night, after the kids have gone to bed, hoping the dishes have cleaned themselves and the laundry will just disappear.

We see you over there, building that dream while raising the kids, managing the house, rocking that full-time career, making time for the people who matter most in your life, and still managing to get the daily to-do list DONE.

You might not realize it but, girl, look at you: DOING THE DARN THING!

Gosh, we wish that we could pull up a chair beside you and tell you that you are doing an incredible job, that all those late night hours and early mornings are your success story in REAL TIME! The story you are writing and your decision to show up consistently is making a real impact on the lives of others.

But since we can't do that, instead we will tell you that we are here on the other side of this planner, rooting for you, cheering for you, believing in you, and knowing that YOU can truly feel good about building your direct sales business the right way!

We know because we were once there, too.

We were exactly where you are, navigating the messy middle of "figuring it out," spending time watching YouTube videos and Googling everything about how to grow a social media following, early in the morning, late into the evening, and in the pockets of time that fit into the rest of our lives.

If we could boil down those eleven years of learning social media into one big idea, it's this: connection.

Everyone craves connection: being heard, being seen, and believing that someone has their back. It's essential to connect to others who are walking through the same struggles that we are and connect with someone who's accomplished great things that we wish to achieve as well.

When it comes to cultivating community, connection is about converting followers into clients, and, most importantly, leaving a lasting impact.

Even on social media where we are more connected than ever before, we can often feel isolated from the world around us. Ever feel like that? We can scroll without pause and catch ourselves going down a rabbit hole of comparison if we aren't careful.

Our vision is to simplify your social strategy and clarify your specific marketing message. This planner is designed to help you do just that.

The Direct Sales Done Right Planner is your personal guide to help you create an intentional and purposeful brand that allows you to stand out in a noisy social media world and connect with those who crave your consistent message.

We've divided this planner into five sections. Before using the planner, we've created an overview on the next page for each section that will help you get the most out of your investment!

> *The people who are crazy enough to think that they can change the world, are the ones who usually do.*
> *-Steve Jobs*

SECTIONS OF THE PLANNER

 ## 1. Social Media Done Right

In direct sales, you likely have two marketing goals for your business:
1. You want to showcase the products and the services you offer.
2. You want to share the business opportunity with others.

This section is a guide and resource designed specifically for women in direct sales to help you clarify your marketing strategy, identify your ideal audience, and convert your prospects into raving clients and team members. We are going to create the content that will help you connect with your audience so that you can confidently sell and recruit.

 ## 2. Vision Casting Done Right

We all love a little "dream big" motivation now and then, but when it comes to making your vision a reality, what's the secret ingredient? If you've ever felt confused by the how-to of vision casting, we've got you covered!

 ## 3. Goal Setting Done Right

Setting clear and defined goals is ESSENTIAL when it comes to creating a solid strategy for your business. With a clear vision of where you want to go, it's time to create the road map that will get you there. In this section, Melanie will go over how to set annual goals that can be broken down into monthly and weekly goals.

 ## 4. Planning Done Right

This section is gold! This is your weekly planner which contains 52 weeks for you to brainstorm your strategy for each week while reflecting on brand growth, messaging, and overall conversion. Here you will review your marketing for the week, break down your weekly stats, and analyze and clarify your messaging.

 ## 5. Confetti!

How about we make your content pop?! Looking to create "wow factor" content? We've devoted an entire section to a few of our favorite direct sales marketing resources that we've created and perfected over the past ten years. This is the confetti for your social media! If you're ever stuck, this is the part of the planner that will help you get unstuck!

5 TIPS TO MAKE YOUR PHOTOS POP!

(iPhone photography done right)

LIGHTING
Use natural lighting as much as possible. Don't take photos in dark rooms. Make sure there is a large intake of light in the room. Don't rely on the filter to fix the photo. Filters aren't always enough to fix a poor-quality photograph.

PRESETS
Using a preset boosts the vibrance and aesthetic colors in your photographs. Presets allow you to create a cohesive and aesthetic theme on IG. Using the same preset on each photo will create the perfect unified theme.

EXPOSURE
Taking a photo that is backlit can diminish features of your face in photos. Be sure to adjust image exposure by touching different areas on your phone you want to be brightened up.

POSES
Different poses work for different people. It is important to switch up your poses in each photo to add a diverse element to your photos. Try posing with colorful props for that extra pop of color.

ANGLE
The biggest misconception is that taking a photo from above makes for a better photo. This only works for certain photos—such as group photos, because it allows for more people to be seen in the photo. If you are taking a photo individually, it is important to utilize side angles and front-facing angles.

INSTAGRAM STORY IDEAS

- Motivational Monday
- Testimonial Tuesday
- Way Back Wednesday
- Throwback Thursday
- Flashback Friday
- Selfie Saturday
- Self Care Sunday
- Sneak Peek At Your Fb Group
- Behind The Scenes Of Your Day
- Using The Direct Sales Done Right Planner
- Listening To The Direct Sales Done Right Podcast
- Celebrate A Win You Had
- Story Behind Your Why
- Share What Makes You Unique
- Favorite Movie
- How You Relax On Weekends
- Favorite Quote
- Business Mentor You Admire
- Favorite Meme
- Would You Rather Using The Poll Feature
- Favorite Ig Account
- Give 3 Business Tips
- Do A Story Takeover With A Guest
- Mini Training
- Share The #1 Faq You Get
- Who Your Ideal Client Is
- Share Your Daily To-Do List
- Favorite Apps
- Share A Stat From Your Industry
- Favorite Personal Development Book

30 DAYS OF BUSINESS POSTS

Share your story:

Before I was _____. Now I am _____.
I got there by _____.

- Share a fear you've overcome.
- Share a lesson you've learned through personal development.
- Share a small financial win.
- Freedom of time post.
- Location of freedom post.
- Share how you've become more confident.
- Share a dream you're working towards.
- Share on how you're working on earning a rewards trip.
- How has the company's community blessed your life?
- What initially attracted you to the business?
- 5 Things you didn't know about me (relate them to the business)
- What initially attracted you to the business?
- Share your process of beginning to pay off debt. {Commit publicly}
- Is this business helping you pay for Christmas in cash?
- Can you go on a date with your spouse and your business pays for it?! Freedom!
- Why I love working from home.
- Working on my terms and not having to report to a boss.
- I make an impact while making an income.
- My income has allowed me to do _____.
- I not only get to help people feel _____ but I also earn amazing rewards for doing my job.
- I never knew that there was another way …
- I don't ever want to look back on my life and wonder, "What if?"
- How I can mentor you …
- Why is my business different from any other?
- What can you expect when you sign up with me?
- Share your vision board. People follow someone who is going somewhere.
- WEEKLY: Share a testimonial.
- WEEKLY: Share a team member's success story.
- Is your business giving you a deeper sense of purpose by changing people's lives?
- Overcome common objections.

3 SECRETS TO *accelerate* your direct sales business

SECRET #1:
YOU ARE WORTHY OF BUILDING THE LIFE & BUSINESS YOU DESIRE!

- Ask yourself: what advice can I give my audience that they could immediately take and apply to there life?
- Find affirmations that make you feel empowered.
- Read daily, and apply one teaching immediately! You Are A Badass by Jen Sincero is a great choice!

SECRET #2:
YOU DO NOT NEED TO HOUND YOUR FRIENDS AND FAMILY FOR SALES.

- Effectively tell your story instead of selling your product.
- Build trust and credibility with your audience by getting to know your followers.
- Speak your truth, and be confident in what you have to offer.

SECRET #3:
YOU DO NOT NEED TO BE ONLINE 24/7 TO BE SUCCESSFUL!

- You need to set healthy boundaries.
- Turn off notifications.
- Use the Chic time blocker to mark your work/family time.

DIRECT SALES
Trip Checklist

Direct Sales trips and events are a great way to showcase your business. Use this checklist to capture the great social content

Photos to Take

- Packing your bags
- Airplane pictures
- Vacation destination
- Photo in front of company logo
- Your team members
- Company parties/events
- Trainings/meetings
- Team activities

Stories to Capture

- How you are feeling
- Being at the airport
- Give a tour of your room
- Go live at a location
- Food and drinks
- Parties
- Any fun activities
- Thoughts when leaving

Videos to Create

- Document your time being away
- How you feel
- Share parties and activities
- Being apart of the company
- Share how others can join
- What are you learning?
- Who wants to be here next year?

Things to Post

- The way you are feeling
- Favorite thing from each day
- Benefits of the community
- Friendships you've made
- Masterminding with others
- Recap your experience
- Company updates

YOU DID IT!
WELCOME TO THE 1% CLUB, FRIEND!

You are here at the end of the planner which means you have planned and executed a full year's worth of social media content. We know without a doubt that you have learned so much through this experience, how could you not? Experience is always the best teacher. You have learned so much about your brand, your voice, and what truly brings you joy in what you do. We have no doubt that the more you continue to plan and create content you are going to continue to reach and impact more people.

As experts in the field of direct sales, we know firsthand how challenging it can be to navigate the ever-changing trends of social media. But you are doing the dang thing and so are we. In January 2019, we launched "Chic Influencer" while still growing our direct sales businesses. There were so many new challenges and hurdles to navigate. We completely understand what it is like to follow your passion in the midst of creating something new. Every single day we were faced with obstacles that required us to fail forward and truly live from a place of "figuring it out."

We did not have ALL the answers, but we refused to NOT FIGURE IT OUT! We know it's not about one perfect post. It's about the consistent act of showing up daily, serving your audience, and creating momentum.

Our mission is to help you bridge the gap from where you are now to where you are called to go. We are rooting for you, and we are in the trenches alongside you every single day.

Your Direct Sales Done Right Mentors,

Melanie Mitro & Katy Ursta

CONTENT CREATION CHECKLIST

When you are writing your posts there are a few essential areas that you want to consider to ensure the success of the post. We have included on each weekly page layout the "content creation checklist". Make sure that every post you write includes the following:

- ☐ Bold tagline
- ☐ Personal connection/story
- ☐ Call to think or a call to act
- ☐ An eye-catching image that matches your story

Every post that you write should always begin and end with this question to yourself: What is the purpose of this piece of content? Am I trying to persuade, inform, entertain, or share thoughts and feelings? You never want to just throw up a post to "check off the box." Content for your social media always serves a purpose. That clarity is essential to your brand's success.

The next set of considerations you want to take into account when creating your posts is the *method of delivery* for the post. There are a couple of different ways you can deliver content on social media platforms. As a content creator, you always want to have a variety of posts. Here are the different types of delivery methods for your posts:

- ☐ Static post aka single image
- ☐ Carousel aka swipeable
- ☐ Reel
- ☐ Video format
- ☐ Quoteable

The goal with every piece of content you create is engaging your audience and keeping them on your account longer. If you are writing a post that has five tips in the caption, you can put each of the five tips on a Canva template and the reader swipes left for each of the five tips. This keeps the reader on your account longer and increases the likelihood that they will share the post for other readers to enjoy. Every time you create a post, you should ask yourself if there's a different way you can share the message so it resonates with your audience, whether they are drawn to watching reels, video content or reading static posts. The bottom line is that VARIETY is the SPICE OF LIFE! Make sure you switch it up consistently.

OUR FAVORITE DIRECT SALES DONE RIGHT PODCAST EPISODES TO SUPPORT YOUR MARKETING GOALS!

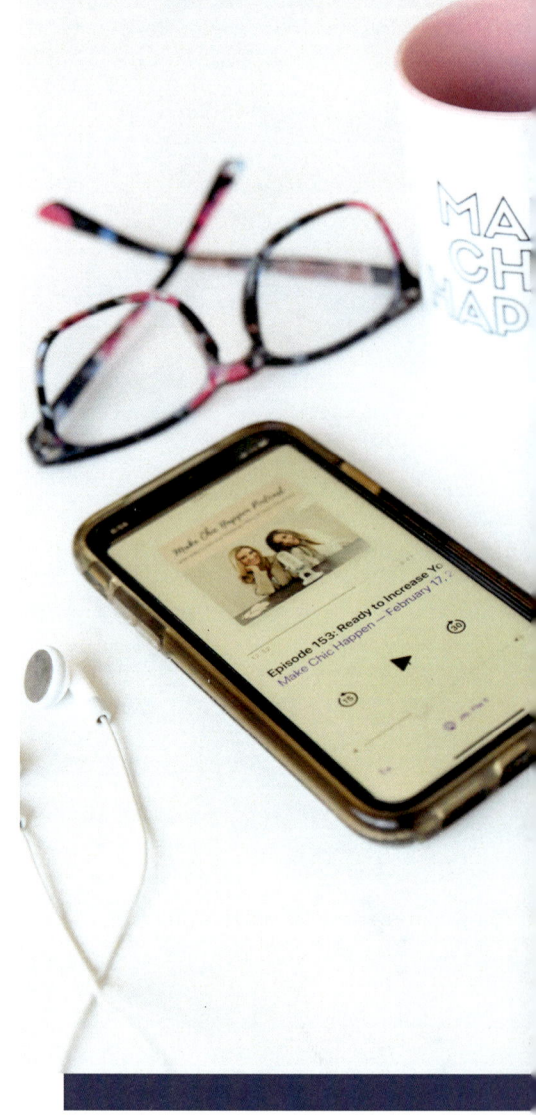

Episode 14: 4 Ways to Position Yourself as an Expert
Episode 102: How to Avoid a "Wing It" Social Media Strategy
Episode 149: Marketing Your Story: A MUST For Every Business Owner
Episode 169: The Direct Sales Standout Part 1
Episode 176: Why Am I Not Getting Results In My Direct Sales Business?
Episode 206: STOP Trying To GROW Your IG Following! DO This Instead!
Episode 224: How Case Studies Can Grow Your Sales and Conversions
Episode 229: How to Actually Hit Your Goals: 5 Steps
Episode 232: How To Create Social Media Content That Supports Your Conversations
Episode 245: The Formula for Social Media Marketing Success

TOP 5 MUST-HAVE APPS TO ROCK INSTAGRAM

Melanie and I get by with a little help from our apps when it comes to ROCKING our Instagram. Here is a list of our favorite apps:

- LightRoom
- Instastories
- Captions
- Repost
- Unfold
- Canva app
- Inshot for video editing
- Apps for your bio link: Milkshake bio, Taplinkbio, and linkinbio

To learn more about how we use each of these apps head over to chicinfluencer.com/free-resources and select *#DirectSalesDoneRight*

Church Resources

Accent on Truth Series

These powerful inductive Bible studies of various books in Scripture encourage students to go deeper in God's Word, embrace its truths and let it change their lives. They include a wealth of profound insights and discussion questions. Based on the KJV.

Encountering the King - Matthew	#28357	0-8963-6307-4
Revealing the Heart of the Servant - Mark	#28365	0-8963-6308-2
Walking with the Son of Man - Luke	#35709	0-8963-6315-5
Knowing the Heart of God - John	#34983	0-8963-6311-2
Learning to Be the Church - Acts	#19844	0-8963-6288-4
Rejoicing in Faith and Freedom - Romans	#19877	0-8963-6292-2
Loving God in a Hostile World - 1 Corinthians	#19885	0-8963-6293-0
Soaring Above Life's Conflicts - 2 Corinthians	#35717	0-8963-6316-3
Defending Christian Liberty - Galatians	#19901	0-8963-6299-X
Fanning the Flames of Light - Ephesians	#19893	0-8963-6298-1
Living Life to the Fullest - Philippians, Colossians & Philemnon	#19851	0-8963-6290-6
Living in Light of the Promise - 1, 2 Thessalonians	#36269	0-8963-6319-8
Growing in Grace and Godliness - 1, 2 Timothy, Titus	#19869	0-8963-6291-4
Knowing the Author of Your Faith - Hebrews	#16691	0-8963-6321-X
Thriving in the Midst of Chaos - James	#19836	0-8963-6287-6
Sharpening Our Eyes of Faith - 1, 2 Peter	#36277	0-8963-6320-1
Loving the World Through Jesus - 1, 2, 3 John, Jude	#34991	0-8963-6312-0
Unwrap Mysteries of Things to Come - Revelation	#15107	0-8963-6322-8

Daughters of the King Series

Inspire women of faith to live fully for their Creator with these encouraging Bible studies. The edifying lessons will instill in them a deeper love and understanding for their call as daughters of the Most High God.

Let Every Mother Rejoice	#16170	0-8963-6325-2
Shadows of Sovereignty	#16188	0-8963-6326-0
Contentment	#19927	0-8963-6294-9
Choices of the Heart	#19968	0-8963-6295-7
My Father in Me	#28381	0-8963-6309-0
At the Heart of Friendship	#54619	0-7814-5555-3
Character of the King	#28399	0-8963-6310-4
Romantic Love: My Father's Gift	#35311	0-8963-6313-9
Whispers from My Heart	#35428	0-8963-6314-7
Celebrating the Heart of the Marriage	#36251	0-8963-6317-1
Women with Courageous Hearts	#36863	0-8963-6318-4
Heart Wisdom	#54601	0-7814-5554-5

Missions Made Fun for Kids

Help children gain a true eternal perspective of the Bible and develop a vision for the importance of missions with this great resource. It will encourage them to realize that every person needs the saving grace of Jesus.
#24604 0-8963-6306-6

Spur-of-the-Moment Books

If you're looking for fun-to-learn and easy-to-teach biblical principles for your students, but don't have a lot of time to brainstorm ideas, this series is for you! With just a few basic supplies on hand, you can provide children with meaningful activities when you need to fill the time.
Spur-of-the-Moment Crafts #21196 . . . 0-8963-6327-9
Spur-of-the-Moment Games and
Learning Activities . . . . #21188 . . . 0-8963-6328-7

Church Time for 2's and 3's

Make a lasting impact on little ones in your children's church with this all-in-one kit related to our Sunday school curriculum. The quarterly packet includes a Let's Sing Motions 'n Music cassette with song sheets and a Leader's Guide containing tons of resources and flexible plans for long or short periods. You can conveniently customize it to meet your needs!
#4018

Church Time for 4's and 5's

You'll ignite young students' hearts with this essential curriculum kit that includes Let's Sing Motions 'n Music cassette, song sheets and self-contained Leader's Guide. It will ease your planning time with an abundance of resources and flexible plans. Also includes reproducible copymasters providing exciting activities and memory verses for applying the Bible Truth.
#4028

The Bible Exposition Commentary V1

Compiled from Dr. Wiersbe's popular "Be" series, the people, places, history and teachings from Matthew through Galatians come to life in this powerful commentary. Contains digestible sections that emphasize personal application and biblical content.
#52902 1-5647-6030-8

The Bible Exposition Commentary V2

Bring the Scriptures to light and gain a better understanding of Ephesians through Revelation with Dr. Wiersbe's "Be" books compiled in this easy-to-read format that encourages personal reflection.
#52910 1-5647-6031-6

To order, call 1-800-323-7543 or 1-800-263-2664 in Canada.
Visit us online at www.accentcurriculum.com or contact your local Christian bookstore.

The harvest is great . . .
The workers are few.

At Accent Bible curriculum, we applaud the efforts of teachers like you who sacrifice their time to sow seeds of God's truth. To assist, we've made it our mission for the last five decades to equip teachers with the right tools to reach your students with the hope and truth of God's Word.

Our comprehensive Sunday school curriculum is Scripturally sound with a baptistic doctrinal emphasis. We use only the King James Version of the Bible in our material and are committed to helping generations stay true to the Word of God.

Accent guarantees a successful classroom experience with a variety of teaching materials. You can customize to meet your students' needs while holding their attention and inspiring your class to learn. We've built our lessons on a three-step plan that helps you prepare your heart to communicate the Bible truth, and help students apply it to their daily lives.

For more information or to receive your free samples, call us today at 1-800-323-7543 or 1-800-263-2664 in Canada. Visit us on the web at www.accentcurriculum.com.

ACCENT
PUBLICATIONS

"Very family-oriented (could relate it to their own families, by example)."
— Carolyn Queen
Sunday school teacher
Pacolet, SC

"I liked the emphasis on the usage of the Scriptures. The format made it easy to teach and in a way my students could understand."
— Colleen Martin
Sunday school teacher
Delavan, IL

We believe in . . .

- *The Trinity of God*
- *The Verbal, Plenary Inspiration of Scripture*
- *The Virgin Birth of Jesus Christ*
- *His Blood Atonement*
- *His Bodily Resurrection*
- *The Personal and Imminent Return of Christ*
- *Personality of Satan*
- *The Autonomy of the Local Church*
  - *Worldwide Missions — the Obligation of Every Church*
    - *The Total Depravity of Natural Man*
    - *Person and Work of the Holy Spirit*
  - *Justification by Faith*
- *The Eternal Security of the Believer*
  - *The Priesthood of the Believer*
  - *The Reality of Heaven and Hell*
    - *Two Ordinances Only: Baptism by Immersion and The Lord's Supper*

ACCENT
PUBLICATIONS

The Curriculum
Inspired by the
Inspired Word

Featuring King James Scriptures Excusively

Accent Sunday school curriculum is unique among resources. Accent reflects an emphasis on baptistic doctrine and a commitment to the verbal and plenary inspiration of Scripture reflected in the King James Version.

Prepare your students to learn and apply God's Word
Accent guarantees a successful classroom experience using a variety of teaching materials that hold the attention of students and inspire each to learn. Materials can be customized to meet particular class needs.

Let the Inspired Word inspire your students with Accent.

Order Your Free Sample Kit Today And We'll Send You:

✔ Teacher's Manual
✔ Teacher's Resources
✔ Student Book
✔ Take-Home Papers

Order Today!

Call: 1-800-323-7543 Fax: 1-800-430-0726
Online: accentcurriculum.com
In Canada: 1-800-263-2664 Fax: 1-800-461-3575

Or visit your local Christian bookstore!

Another fine curriculum from **Cook**
COMMUNICATIONS
MINISTRIES

"Discovering Jesus as Your Savior."

Use the other side of this page to talk with kids who express interest in discovering Jesus as Savior. See Page D•9 for more about this resource.

STEP 1 This is the necessary first step. Sorrow for our sin is appropriate (*2 Corinthians 7:10*). God loves us even though we sin (*Romans 5:8*). We must recognize that we deserve God's punishment and His love is a free gift. (*Romans 6:23*)

STEP 2 We must truly believe in God and want to be forgiven by Him (*Hebrews 11:6*). Without sincere desire, we will not find God.

STEP 3 We must declare our belief in Jesus and God's gift of salvation (*Romans 10:9-10*). Without belief there is no forgiveness.

STEP 4 Asking in words that are meaningful to us is required. Once we ask in faith, we can celebrate new life in Christ and trust in God's faithfulness (*1 John 1:9*).

STEP 5 Reading the Bible, praying, and coming to church to learn about God are ways to learn more. God wants us to "grow in the grace and knowledge of our Lord and Savior Jesus Christ" (*2 Peter 3:18*).

STEP 6 It is important to let children express their decision in their own words. It will ensure that they understand what has happened and prepare them to share the Good News with others. Jesus teaches us to tell others about Him (*Matthew 10:32; 28:19*).

Dear Parent,

Today at VBS your child expressed their desire to accept Jesus Christ as Lord and Savior. After hearing the Bible truths and explanations printed on the other side of this paper, your child responded to the questions presented and prayed for salvation.

Please give your child the opportunity to tell you about his or her decision in his or her own words. The following questions may help guide your conversation.

- *Why did you decide to ask Jesus to be your Savior?*
- *What does this decision mean to you?*
- *How will you learn more about Jesus and what He wants you to do?*
- *Do you have any questions right now about God, or what it means to believe in Jesus as your Savior?*

If you'd like help answering your child's questions, talk with the leaders of the church where your child is attending VBS.

If you are seeking God's free gift of salvation for yourself, the leaders and members of the church where your child attends VBS would be happy to talk with you about how to receive forgiveness and become part of God's family.

Discovering Jesus As Your Savior

1
God loves us but He does not like our sin. The Bible teaches that all people have sinned or disobeyed God. (Romans 3:23)

Have you sinned by disobeying God?

2
The Bible says that our sin separates us from God (Romans 6:23). There is only one way that we can be connected to God and live with Him forever. We must be forgiven by God.

Do you want to know how to be forgiven by God?

3
Jesus has made the way for us to be forgiven by God. Jesus is God's perfect Son. Jesus died on a cross to take the consequences for our sins. (John 3:16) Because Jesus died for us, our sins can be forgiven.

Do you believe that Jesus died on the cross to forgive you of your sins?

4
Jesus didn't stay dead. The Bible tells us that He rose from the dead and is alive today. So we can talk to Him right now. If we believe that Jesus died on the cross to take the consequences for our sins (Romans 10:9-10), we can ask Him to forgive us of our sins. The Bible promises that if we ask Jesus to forgive us, He will. (1 John 1:9)

Would you like to ask Jesus to forgive you of your sins?

5
Once we have asked Jesus to forgive us, our sins are forgiven. Jesus saves us from the result of our sins. When we trust Jesus as our Savior, we are part of God's family forever. (1 John 5:11-12)

Because we are part of His family, we are to live in ways that please God and do things that help us learn more about Him. (Colossians 1:10)

What are some ways you can learn more about Jesus?

6
Now that you are forgiven and part of God's family (John 1:12), you will want to share your decision with others.

With whom will you share your decision to trust Jesus as your Savior?

CONFETTI

Take your marketing to the next level with these resources!

20 CONTENT STARTERS

It's ok if you are lacking creativity. It doesn't always come naturally to us either. If you need to create a post or reel but you just aren't feeling it, simply use these content ideas to get your creativity flowing.

- Product Spotlight: Showcase one of your favorite products and explain why you love it.
- Behind-the-Scenes: Give your audience a sneak peek into your daily routine or how you manage your business.
- Customer Testimonials: Share a success story or testimonial from a satisfied customer.
- Motivational Quotes: Post an uplifting quote related to entrepreneurship or personal growth.
- Transformation Tuesday: Share a before-and-after photo or story related to your products/journey.
- FAQs and Q&A: Answer common questions about common struggles of your ideal client.
- Tip of the Day: Offer a useful tip related to your niche or industry.
- Day in the Life: Document a typical day in your life, showing how you balance work and personal activities.
- Host a Giveaway: Encourage engagement by running a giveaway related to your products.
- Share Your Story: Open up about your journey in network marketing, including challenges and victories.
- Client Case Study: Highlight a loyal customer or team member and share their success story. Make sure to highlight their pain points prior to working with you and how you helped him/her resolve their struggle!
- Before-and-After Results: Showcase the tangible results of using your products.
- Team Appreciation: Recognize and appreciate your team members or downline for their hard work.
- Educational Content: Provide valuable information about product you love that also compliments what you sell!
- Live Demo or Tutorial: Host a live session demonstrating how to use your products effectively.
- Book/Resource Recommendations: Share books or resources that have helped you in your journey as an entrepreneur.
- Flash Sale or Limited-Time Offer: Create a sense of urgency by promoting a special offer.
- Collaboration: Knowing a pain point of your audience go live with someone who can give tips/advice to your audience!
- Personal Growth Reflection: Share a personal development insight or milestone that has contributed to your success.
- Testimonials from Team Members: Share success stories from members of your team, highlighting their achievements.

Remember to add a personal touch to each post, and engage with your audience in the comments section to foster a sense of community and trust. These content ideas should help you provide value and showcase your expertise in the network marketing or direct sales field.

confetti!

5